Modern Pagan Prayers

Lucía Moreno-Velo and Gwyneth Box

Turn of the wheel

A year of modern Pagan prayer and praise

© Lucía Moreno-Velo & Gwyneth Box

Texts: Lucía Moreno-Velo & Gwyneth Box

Book design: Tantamount

First published July 2021

All rights reserved. No part of this publication may be reproduced, distributed, transmitted, or stored in a database or retrieval system, in any form or by any means, without the prior written permission of the authors.

To the Old Crone that spins the wheel,
making sure one season comes after
the other, in perfect order.

And to my children, who make
all this spinning feel like a blur.

LMV

To Miss Roberts, Mrs Inggs,
Mr Fitzmaurice, Miss Nichols,
Mrs Pearce, Mrs Parkes, Miss Vigus,
Miss McNaughton and all the other
teachers who sowed the seeds of
wonder in a child's mind and made
this project possible.

GEB

We offer you these prayers for your own adaptation

The prayers, songs and other pieces contained in this book are made available for you to adapt to suit your own circumstances and devotions. Although each of the prayers is complete as is, you may choose to alter or add details to bring them in line with your personal experience and situation – perhaps simply changing pronouns to suit a single or plural voice as appropriate, perhaps adjusting details to more closely match your own environment.

You may also prefer to use only fragments of some of the pieces, to divide the readings between different voices, or to include actions to illustrate and accompany the prayers.

We suggest you turn this book into a keepsake for the future. Just record your favorite ways to celebrate each festival in the "My Wheel of the Year" section at the end of the book. Use this space to write your own prayers, recipes, activities and family traditions. There is also a short space at the end of each festival for notes.

The Wheel of the Year

The Wheel of the Year is a 20th century creation that conflates many different holidays and traditions, some with historical basis, others not so much. Originally Wiccan, it is now widely followed by many Pagans in some form or another. Of course, you are under no obligation to celebrate these festivals in any fixed way, or at all. You may substitute all or some of the holidays for celebrations of your own, or add any other that might have religious or secular significance for you. The possibilities are endless! We do find, however, that repeating the same celebrations in the same, or similar, ways year after year can deepen our understanding and create wonderful traditions.

The Wheel of the Year consists of eight holidays called Sabbats. These are divided into the so-called Lesser Sabbats and Greater Sabbats. The Lesser Sabbats are the equinoxes and the solstices, the calendar points that mark the position of the Earth in relation to the Sun. The Greater Sabbats fall at approximately regular intervals between these.

Because the Wheel of the Year marks the journey of the Earth around the Sun and the procession of the seasons, many cultures and religions around the world celebrate festivals on similar dates – although it's important to realise that two holidays that fall at the same time may be honoring or celebrating very different things. The astronomical connection also explains why the holidays fall on the opposite days of the calendar in the Southern and Northern hemispheres. The solar events can drift a few days each year, which means the festivals are not actually fixed. The dates when people celebrate depend on their tradition, their ancestral culture and their personal preference.

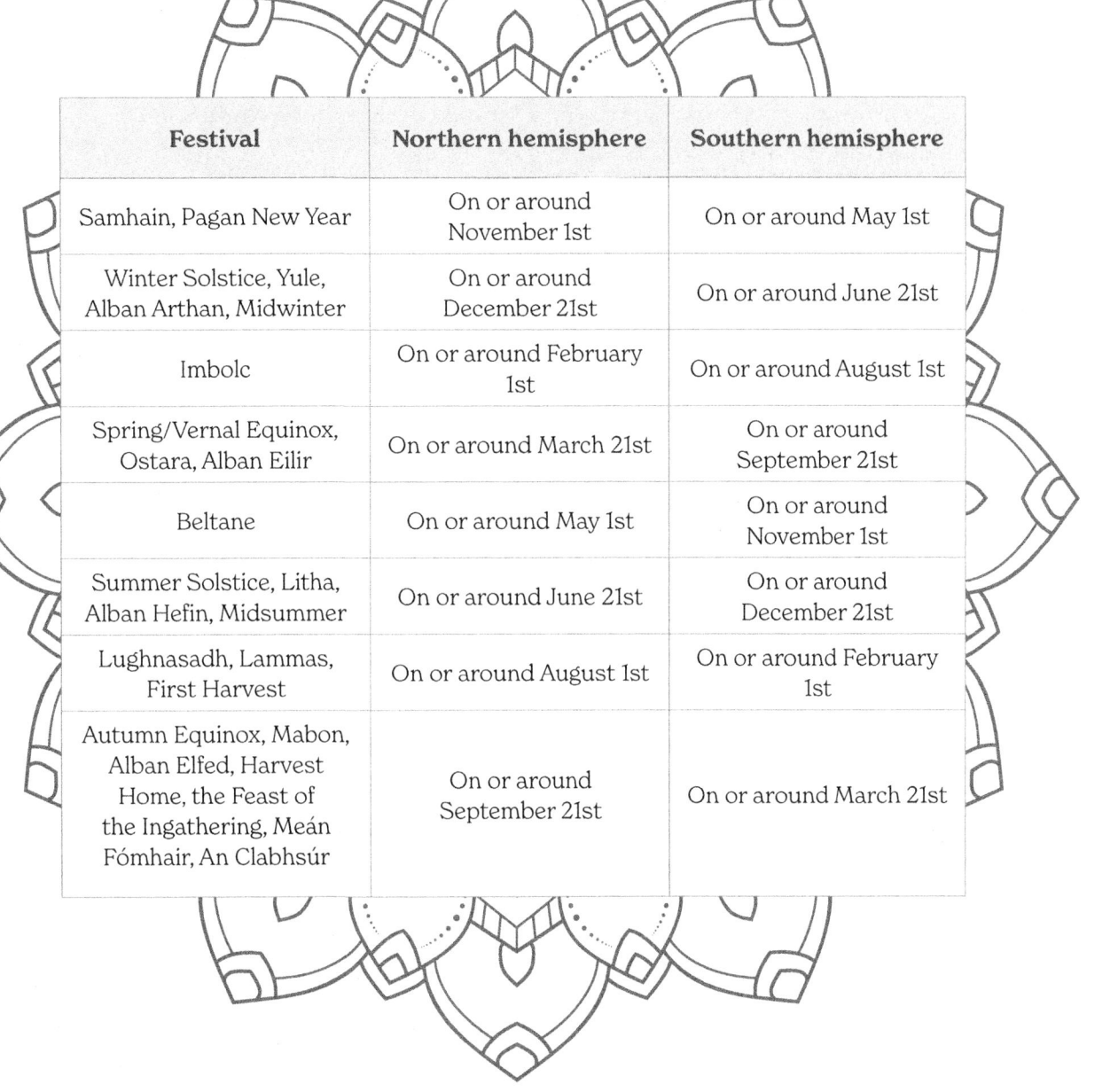

Festival	Northern hemisphere	Southern hemisphere
Samhain, Pagan New Year	On or around November 1st	On or around May 1st
Winter Solstice, Yule, Alban Arthan, Midwinter	On or around December 21st	On or around June 21st
Imbolc	On or around February 1st	On or around August 1st
Spring/Vernal Equinox, Ostara, Alban Eilir	On or around March 21st	On or around September 21st
Beltane	On or around May 1st	On or around November 1st
Summer Solstice, Litha, Alban Hefin, Midsummer	On or around June 21st	On or around December 21st
Lughnasadh, Lammas, First Harvest	On or around August 1st	On or around February 1st
Autumn Equinox, Mabon, Alban Elfed, Harvest Home, the Feast of the Ingathering, Meán Fómhair, An Clabhsúr	On or around September 21st	On or around March 21st

For many Pagans, the year starts and ends at Samhain. For others, it starts at Yule and ends at Samhain; for these people, the time between Samhain and Yule is called the Dead (or Fallow) Time. Although less well known than other Wheel of the Year milestones, we have chosen to include the Dead Time in this book.

The book title reminds us that year follows year in a continuous cycle, so, although we have chosen to open with "New Beginnings", there is no corresponding ending piece. As the musicians say, "da capo".

New beginnings	1
Samhain	4
A prayer to the Beloved Dead	6
A prayer to the Washer of Shrouds	8
Invitation to a dumb supper	10
Hymn to the Maiden	12
To the Goddess in her grossness	14
The dead time	18
A prayer to those who hunt our nights	20
Sacrifice	22
I know	24
A prayer to the Star of the Sea	26
Song of the wild	28
Yule	32
A prayer to the Queen of Yule	34
Vigil	36
The world turns towards the light	37
Small things	38
In praise of Sol Invictus	40
Imbolc	44
I prepare for the coming light	46
Welcome	47
An offering to Brighid	48
The song that the world sings	50
Well blessing	52

Ostara — 56

- In praise of swallows — 58
- Springsong for Demeter — 60
- Calling the hare — 62
- The world rejoices — 64
- Spring prayer — 65

Beltane — 68

- Beacon song — 70
- Song for the May Queen — 72
- Beltane tryst — 74
- Dedication — 75
- Teach me the words — 76

Litha — 80

- Song for the shortest night — 82
- Salutation — 83
- A witch's litany — 84
- A prayer to the ocean waves — 86
- A solstice request — 88

Lammas — 92

- My Lady's cloak — 94
- Stories — 95
- In honor of Lugh of the Long Hand — 96
- Kitchen witch — 98
- Trimming the dead wood — 100

Mabon — 104

- As we approach the new school year — 106
- The world slips towards darkness — 107
- To Rosmerta, the Most Providential — 108
- The fruit of wisdom — 110
- Harvest song for the Goddess — 112

New beginnings

The door shuts on the old year
and the new year lies ahead.
As new roads unwind before me,
I pause to take stock:

I gather to me the earth, whose paths I tread;
I hold her in my thoughts and cherish her.
May I respect and honor her gifts at all times,
never taking for granted the bounty she offers.

I gather to me the sky and all the celestial bodies;
I hold them in my thoughts and cherish them.
May I never cease to wonder at their mysteries,
welcoming sunlight, starlight and moonlight with equal joy.

I gather to me my friends and family;
I hold them in my thoughts and cherish them.
May I ease their journey whenever possible
and be a good and faithful companion to those I travel with.

I gather to me all strangers, plants and animals;
I hold them in my thoughts and cherish them.
May I recognize their place in this shared space
and be tolerant and fair-minded whenever our ways cross.

I gather to me my own body;
I hold it in my thoughts and cherish it.
I know its strengths and weaknesses
and grant myself permission to forgive.

I gather to me my own spirit;
I hold it in my thoughts and cherish it.
I own its secrets and its power
and vow to uphold its promise.

The door shuts on the old year
and the new year lies ahead.
New roads unwind before me
and I greet this new adventure
with all its rewards and challenges.
I gather it into my thoughts;
I hold it in my mind and cherish it.
And I step out on this journey
with gratitude and confidence.

Samhain

A prayer to the Beloved Dead

A prayer to the Washer of Shrouds

Invitation to a dumb supper

Hymn to the Maiden

To the Goddess in her grossness

A prayer to the Beloved Dead

Walk with me,
Beloved Dead;
do not let go of my hand.
With you, I am fearless.
Guide my path.

In my dealings with the world,
guide my path.

In conflict and in peace,
in scarcity and in abundance,
in uncertainty and in clarity,
in danger and in safety,
in chaos and in calm,
with you, I am fearless.
Guide my path.

In the lows and in the highs of life,
guide my path.

In courage and in fear,
in elation and in despair,
in happiness and in sadness,
in wisdom and in ignorance,
in company and in solitude,
with you, I am fearless.
Guide my path.

In every moment of my journey,
guide my path.

In the morning and in the evening,
in light and in darkness,
in sunshine and in rain,
in youth and in old age,
in summer and in winter,
with you, I am fearless.
Guide my path.

In life and after life,
and at every turn
of my existence,
walk with me,
Beloved Dead;
do not let go of my hand.
With you, I am fearless.
Guide my path.

A prayer to the Washer of Shrouds

> *"from me all things proceed,*
> *and unto me must all things return"*
> *The Charge of the Goddess*
> — D. Valiente

Lady of the Creek,
Washer of Shrouds,
whose death do you foretell?

You swirl white linen in the water,
unmoved by the cold;
you cast it in the air, like a net.

Lady of the Creek,
Catcher of Souls,
who are you singing for?

You are in the stories of my people,
the tales whispered by firelight,
while, behind us, shadows listen.

Lady of the Creek,
Sower of the Seeds of Life,
whose life will you harvest?

You give birth to all
and will give death to all in turn;
shrouds and swaddling bands tangle in the wash.

Lady of the Creek,
Mother of All,
who will you embrace?

You care for all; you welcome all:
the polyp, the tiger, the roach,
the oak and the mayfly.

Lady of the Creek,
known by many other names,
you hold me in your hands.
Blessed be the fragility
that will bring me back to you at the end.

Invitation to a dumb supper

Heed my call, all you who hunger
for the warmth of hearth and home
and earthly life.

Wanderers in this realm,
you who doubted at the threshold
and chose to remain among us,
hear me.

Inhabitants of the liminal,
of dark, cold corners,
unknown and unnamed,
hear me.

Spirits of the land,
wild folk of the old tales,
quiet neighbors and friends,
hear me.

Come forward
and rest a while at my side.
Take this offering.

Tonight the veil is lifted
and I welcome you,
on this holy night,
into my home.

Let us break bread together.

Hymn to the Maiden

Beloved Lady,
rest, now, and gather your strength.
Withdraw to the halls of your Lord,
where the flowers are cold crystal
and the walls glisten black.
Rest, now, and gather your strength.

Beloved Lady,
rest, now, and gather your strength,
safe in the halls of your Lord,
where the sound of the hammer and anvil
rings out like a bell.
Rest, now, and gather your strength.

Beloved Lady,
rest, now, and gather your strength,
deep in the halls of your Lord,
though your mother wanders above
bewailing her loss.
Rest, now, and gather your strength.

We await your return in the springtime:
come to us then, decked in green;
bring us joy and new life,
bring us proof of renewal.
Rest, now, and gather your strength,
beloved Lady.

To the Goddess in her grossness

*With warm thanks
to John Halstead,
the Allergic Pagan*

Praise to the Goddess in her grossness

*In blood and wine,
in milk and sap,
in oil and brine,
we praise her*

Let us praise her liquid fecundity
in the hidden waters of the womb,
in bloody menstrual rags and viscous afterbirth,
in sodden mulch and in the slow ooze and suck of mud,
in swamps, in rock pools, and in the teeming ocean.

*In blood and wine,
in milk and sap,
in oil and brine,
we praise her*

Let us praise her patient reclamation
in the black soot and filigree of household mold,
in the writhe of earthworms and scurry of woodlice,
in the scouring tongues of rain and wind,
in the bleaching heat, and in the creep of rising tides.

In blood and wine,
in milk and sap,
in oil and brine,
we praise her

Let us praise her impartial brutality
in the remorseless pursuit of predators,
in the slip and shock of tectonic plates,
in the silent mists of spores and viruses,
and in the toxic fumes and putrescence of landfills.

In blood and wine,
in milk and sap,
in oil and brine,
we praise her.

My Samhain

The dead time

A prayer to those who hunt our nights

Sacrifice

I know

A prayer to the Star of the Sea

Song of the wild

A prayer to those who hunt our nights

Unknown but not unnamed,
Wild Hunt, Ghost Riders,
Santa Compaña,
riding through the centuries,
down the mountainside
and through the air,
I see you.

Though many fear you, I honor you
and ask you to grant me strength and wisdom
to look death in the eye.

They say you ride,
crashing through the forest,
howling among clouds,
wailing and screaming,
so that many fear the sight of you.

But this I know:
you can also be seen, patient, quiet,
waiting on the riverbank
or where the field meets the thicket,
dressed in white, holding on to each other
for dear life, or death,
a welcoming committee
for those of us who have lived enough.

Though many fear you, I honor you,
and ask you to grant me strength and wisdom
to look death in the eye.

May I never fear your welcome,
but close my eyes in respect
while you pass me by,
until the night I must open them,
and then, do so with honor,
knowing it is among you
that I belong.

Sacrifice

The rising sun bruises cloud on the mountains
Flaxen-haired Giver, *Lady of the Slain*

Mist scarves the air; white as a winding sheet
Soothsayer, Truthsayer, *blessed be thy name*

Hollow grapes rattle, hanging black on the vine
Flaxen-haired Giver, *Lady of the Slain*

Brittle earth splinters under our purblind feet
Soothsayer, Truthsayer, *blessed be thy name*

Our throats constrict; each breath tastes of metal
Flaxen-haired Giver *Lady of the Slain*

We gurn at the cold, blear-eyed and yawning
Soothsayer, Truthsayer, *blessed be thy name*

A blade cuts the air; a pig's squeal is silenced
Flaxen-haired Giver, *Lady of the Slain*

Blood flows red in the white of your morning
Soothsayer, Truthsayer, *blessed be thy name*

Flaxen-haired Giver, *Lady of the Slain*
Soothsayer, Truthsayer, *blessed be thy name*

I know

I know of the stillness,
the quiet moment
before dusk
when the sun shines bright
and night is unimaginable.

I know of the setting of the sun,
sudden, violent,
bleeding on sky and clouds,
heralding a darkness
like no other.

I know of darkness,
of course,
of tunneling silence
at whose door
you must check all hope.

I know of footsteps
and hesitation,
of fear and stubbornness,
of traveling when
there is nothing but the path.

I know, finally, of dawn,
of suns rising
above mausoleums,
of dew dressing flowers
and webs alike.

I know of all of these things
and still I learn.
Every day
brings fresh pain
and fresh pleasure.

A prayer to the Star of the Sea

Hail, Sacred Beacon, Guide for the Lost,
other landmarks have failed and left me adrift;
may you always shine your hope on me.

Tiny pinprick in the dark sky,
you hide the magnitude of your quiet strength;
may you always shine your compassion on me.

You shone on those long gone,
and shine today on all the living;
may you shine, too, on those who will take my place.

For you have seen
suffering and joy,
life and death,
song and wailing,
purpose and madness,

and we have made you offerings
of garlands and lanterns,
fruit and perfume,
souls and bodies,
gold and porcelain.

Hail, Star of the Sea,
suspended above your rocking mirror,
shine your light on me,
for I have lost my way
and long for home.

Song of the wild

Long ago, we danced in the belly of the wolf-mother. In pulsing dark, we danced an ancient dance; in darkness together, brothers, sisters, cousins... gray and gold and red. We counted our steps to the beat of the bitch-wolf's heart. Long ago, we danced in darkness, danced away and down through generations.

Born into the dark den, we cry,
worrying at our mother's teats;
draggled and whimpering, we seek
the milk that frees our voices from the past.

On the moor, we scream our story to the winds.
In the forest, we weave our tales from tree to tree.
From the mountaintop, we cast an echoing net –
yelp and yip and yowl – across the valley.

We laugh in the sunlight, we howl at the moon.
This is our land; we boast our past.
You are family; we declare our kin.
This is our land; we claim our future.

Before our birth, we danced.
We were born into the world to sing.

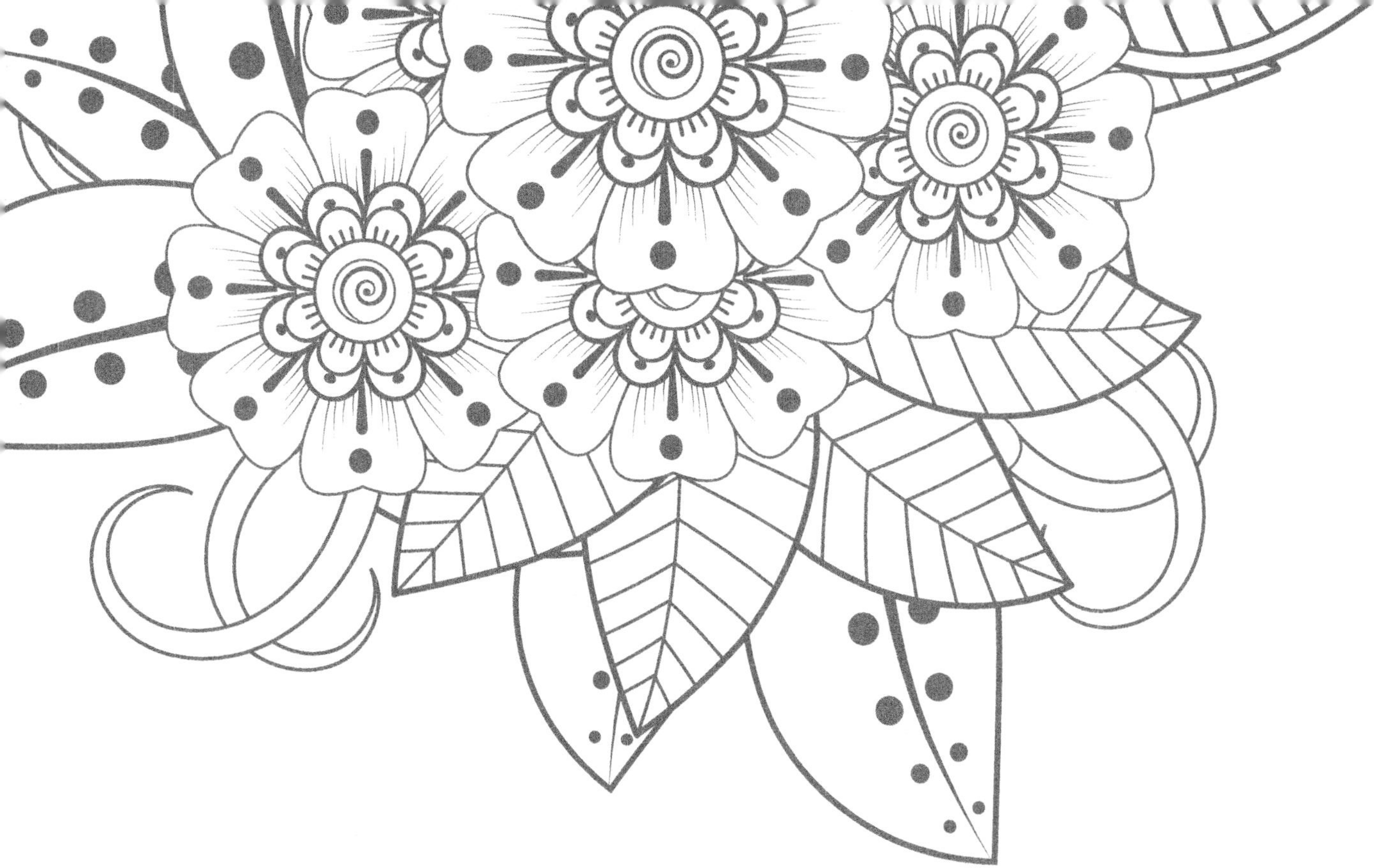

My Dead Time

Yule

A prayer to the Queen of Yule

Vigil

The world turns towards the light

Small things

In praise of Sol Invictus

A prayer to the Queen of Yule

Lady of Light,
Queen of Yule,
come to us in the longest night;
remind us of your promise.

Lady of Light,
known by many names,
come to us crowned in light.
When the year is at its darkest,
bring the promise
of snowdrops and lilacs,
almond blossom and daffodils.

We will give you holly,
mistletoe and spruce.

Lady of Light,
known through the land,
come to us clad in snow.
When the cold is at its sharpest,
bring the promise
of apples and peaches,
of roses, peppers and peas.

We will give you ginger,
cinnamon and mulled wine.

Lady of Light,
known of old,
come to us bearing gifts.
When the land is at its quietest,
bring the promise
of fireworks and fanfare,
barbecues, pomp and parade.

We will give you song,
good cheer and celebration.

Lady of Light,
Queen of Yule,
come to us in the longest night;
remind us of your promise.
Already, deep in the earth,
at the bottom of rivers,
and inside cold wood,
a new year is quickening.

Vigil

We do not fear the dark
for we were born of darkness
and, one day, we will return.

We follow the wheel as it turns.

The turn of the wheel has drawn us
deeper, deeper into the darkness.
The days are short and the nights are long.

We follow the wheel as it turns.

The nights are long and we tire of the dark.
Now, the sun has paused in the heavens;
must we go deeper still into the darkness?

We follow the wheel as it turns.

Born of darkness, we crave the light.
We watch the silent horizon:
may the sun return and banish the dark.

We follow the wheel as it turns.

The world turns towards the light

The world turns towards the light.
The dark nights of winter shorten.
The glad days brighten.

In winter, we hunker down and wait;
we save our energies; we pray
for patience and strength to endure.

In the cold and dark, we watch,
alert for shadows in the darkness,
and listen for birdsong to break the silence.

On the short days, we look
for plant shoots in the dirt
and new growth on old wood.

On the long dark nights, we remember
the past and dream of the future
as the world turns towards the light.

As the world turns towards the light,
the dark nights shorten
and the glad days blaze with hope.

Small things

Small things matter;
small things make a difference.

Small things hold a promise of the future:
    scarlet holly berries;
    the fallen acorn in its leathern cup;
    the egg in the womb.

Small things flavor my wintertime:
    the warm spice in ginger snaps;
    chocolate shards on cappuccino froth;
    the six-edged taste of snowflakes.

Small things brighten my wintertime:
    fairy lights glimpsed between half-closed curtains;
    the dance and spark of an open fire;
    glittering stars in the clear night sky.

Small things touch my heart in winter:
    mistletoe kisses;
    a letter from a loved one;
    the sticky hand of a toddler.

Small things echo through my wintertime:
    the sudden trill of a robin redbreast;
    the scrunch and rustle of wrapping paper;
    voices raised in age-old song.

Small things perfume my wintertime:
    pine needles crushed underfoot;
    the sharp edge of frost in the air;
    the familiar kitchen scents of home.

Small things hold a reminder of hope:
    a smile on a stranger's face;
    a candle in the darkness;
    shared laughter.

In this great universe,
mine is but one small life.
May my small life make a difference.

In praise of Sol Invictus

I glorify the unconquerable sun,
light of our world,
source of all life.

Though the earth lies sleeping,
forest, field and garden, hushed,
yet we will all see him
rising from the snow.

Come, Sol Invictus,
biding your time,
tonight is the solstice,
tomorrow you rise.

Though the bear is in hiding,
geese and storks have flown,
yet we will all see him
rising in the dawn.

Come, Sol Invictus,
biding your time,
tonight is the solstice,
tomorrow you rise.

Though the trees stand naked
and the briar is bare,
yet we will all see him
rising from the land.

Come, Sol Invictus,
biding your time,
tonight is the solstice,
tomorrow you rise.

I glorify the unconquerable sun,
light of our world,
source of all life,
rising among us,
giving us hope.
Tonight is the solstice;
tomorrow he'll return.

My Yule

Imbolc

I prepare for the coming light

Welcome

An offering to Brighid

The song that the world sings

Well blessing

I prepare for the coming light

I sweep winter dark from my home,
clear cobwebs from forgotten corners
and throw away unnecessary clutter.
I launder, mend, iron and fold.

I prepare for the coming light

I look back on the year just gone,
review the high spots and the low;
I make a garland of achievements
and leave the rest behind without remorse.

I prepare for the coming light

I acknowledge my bond to self,
to family, to society and to the gods.
I renew my pledge to self-discovery;
my eyes open to hope.

I prepare for the coming light.

Welcome

Welcome to the child

She walks through fields of silver.
Winter cracks under her feet
and the earth breathes
gossamer. In her wake,
the path is damp
and green.

Welcome to the child

An offering to Brighid

Holy Maiden,
Guardian of the Land,
Champion of the Newly Born,
poet and healer,
Lady of the Forge,
hear my voice in the winter silence.

I come to you with a heart full of joy
and hands full of offerings.
Take these early flowers,
this milk, these moon-shaped cakes.

For you, I sing songs old and new.
May your voice be always in mine.

For you, I braid crosses and straw dolls.
May you find rest in my home.

For you, I bless wells and fountains.
May you gift my loved ones with health.

For you, I light an eternal flame.
May my heart shine with your radiance.

Take these moon-shaped cakes,
this milk, these early flowers.

Heal my wounds and those of my people.
Fill our hearts with song
and our homes with abundance.
Bless the child and the lamb
and the land that sustains them.

Holy Brighid,
Guardian of the Land,
Champion of the Newly Born,
poet and healer,
Lady of the Forge,
hear my voice in the cold silence.

The song that the world sings

"Y el canto del mundo, que es mi propio canto"
— Violeta Parra

At Imbolc the world clears her throat
and readies herself for a new song.

    She tries out her voice
    in the creak and crack of ice
    and in the clear tones
    of snowdrop bells.

    She hums a lullaby
    in the soft flurry of snow,
    each unique note
    blending in harmony.

    She sings out
    in the glint of frost on cars
    and in the sweet melody
    of new green shoots.

She shouts aloud
in the rush of meltwater
and in the dazzle
of dancing rainbows.

At Imbolc the world clears her throat
and readies herself for a new song.
I, too, sing out the joy of renewal
for the world's song is my song.

Well blessing

Hear me, spirit of this well:
I come to you in peace
to honor the sacred nature of this place.

Through many winters and summers
you have provided for all with generosity.

Yours is the spot where the lamb and the bee gather,
where the frog and the violet sing together,
where the traveller sits to rest.

Well of sacred waters, let me honor you:
let me dress you with ribbons and flowers;
let me sing to you sweet tunes and dance around you;
let me bless the land that surrounds you and the water within.

Hear me, spirit of this well:
I leave you in peace, as I came;
I honor and respect you;
you are sacred.

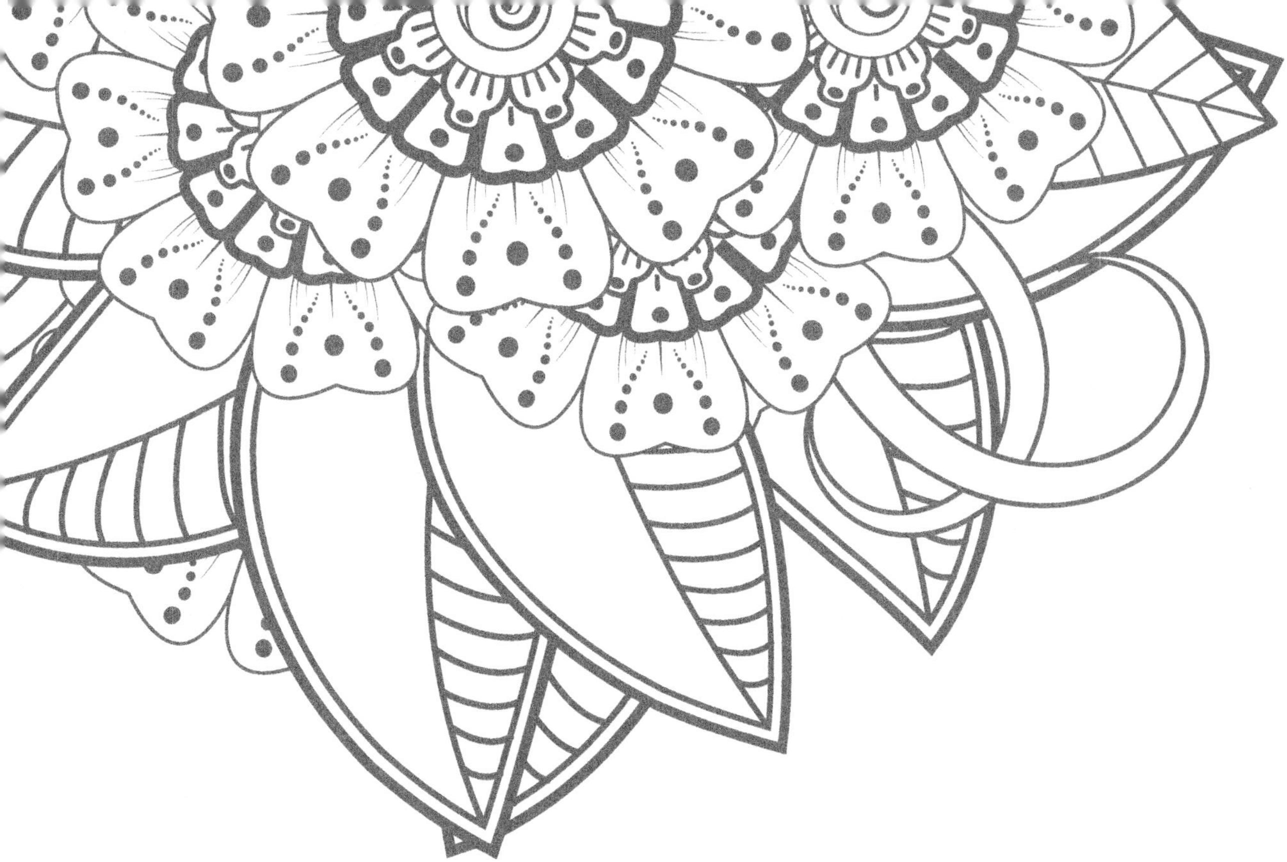

My Imbolc

Ostara

In praise of swallows

Springsong for Demeter

Calling the hare

The world rejoices

Spring prayer

In praise of swallows

Welcome to you, feathered travelers;
we see you and our joy rises up to greet you.

    First one, then two, and then too quick to count,
    you skim the earth; you sail on air.
    You come to set up camp among us once again.

    High above us, your swooping silhouettes
    announce the turning of the year.
    You free our minds from dusty winter thought.

    The smooth arc of your wings
    cuts the air in constant chase.
    You write our future onto the blank page of the sky.

    You sweep upwards, peak, tip turn
    and dive in a single moment.
    You feed on those that plague our summers.

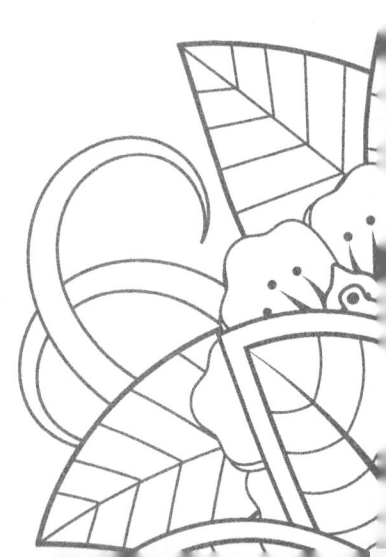

You fly tirelessly, glide and swoop
   without pause or thought of rest.
   You fill our days with movement and laughter.

Come, people of the sky: we give you welcome;
we have held a place for you in our hearts all winter.

Springsong for Demeter

Rejoice, Demeter,
for your daughter returns
from the cold dark halls of the Underworld

Rejoice, Demeter,
for your daughter returns:
welcome her with birdsong and blossom

    Rejoice, Demeter,
    for your daughter returns.
    We welcome her with garlands and posies

    Rejoice, Demeter,
    for your daughter returns.
    We welcome her with music and laughter

Rejoice, Demeter,
for your daughter returns.
We welcome her with dances and drumming

Rejoice, Demeter,
for your daughter returns:
welcome her with birdsong and blossom

Rejoice, Demeter,
for your daughter returns
from the cold dark halls of the Underworld.

Calling the hare

Sweet, sweet hare,
mirrored on the moon,
come from field and meadow,
for I am calling you.

Come, swift messenger,
with news of the spring;
usher in blossom and green shoot,
for I am calling you.

Come, wise guide,
full of ancient art;
open my perception,
for I am calling you.

Come, old alchemist,
with your magic touch;
bring your transformation,
for I am calling you.

Come, mad trickster,
with your ecstatic dance;
give my spirit freedom,
for I am calling you.

Come, sweet hare,
mirrored on the moon;
leap over the winter,
for I am calling you.

The world rejoices

Crocus flames flicker through the grass like wildfire
The Goddess is returning

Daffodil trumpets sound the good tidings abroad
The Goddess is returning

Tulips raise their jewel-bright goblets high – ruby, amber, gold –
The Goddess is returning

Anemones twirl and flounce their ballet skirts in the breeze
The Goddess is returning

Violets and periwinkles whisper in the secret dark
The Goddess is returning

Primroses raise their pale faces to the sun
The Goddess is returning

We, too, put on our best clothes; we gather together and rejoice;
we give thanks with candles and wine, music and dancing;
we whisper the news, we shout it aloud, we raise our faces
to greet the Goddess in all the floral glory of her spring.

Spring prayer

As the sap rises through tree trunks and branches,
bringing renewed vigor to the dull wood,
so, too, let the earth's energy flow inside me,
readying me for new projects and endeavors.

As roots reach down deep into the dark earth
and green shoots push up towards the light,
so, too, let me find sustenance and stability
and let my inspiration rise up into action.

As leaf buds swell and burst with new life
and flower buds unfurl their rainbow petals,
so let my projects grow and blossom,
bringing hope and joy to the world.

My Ostara

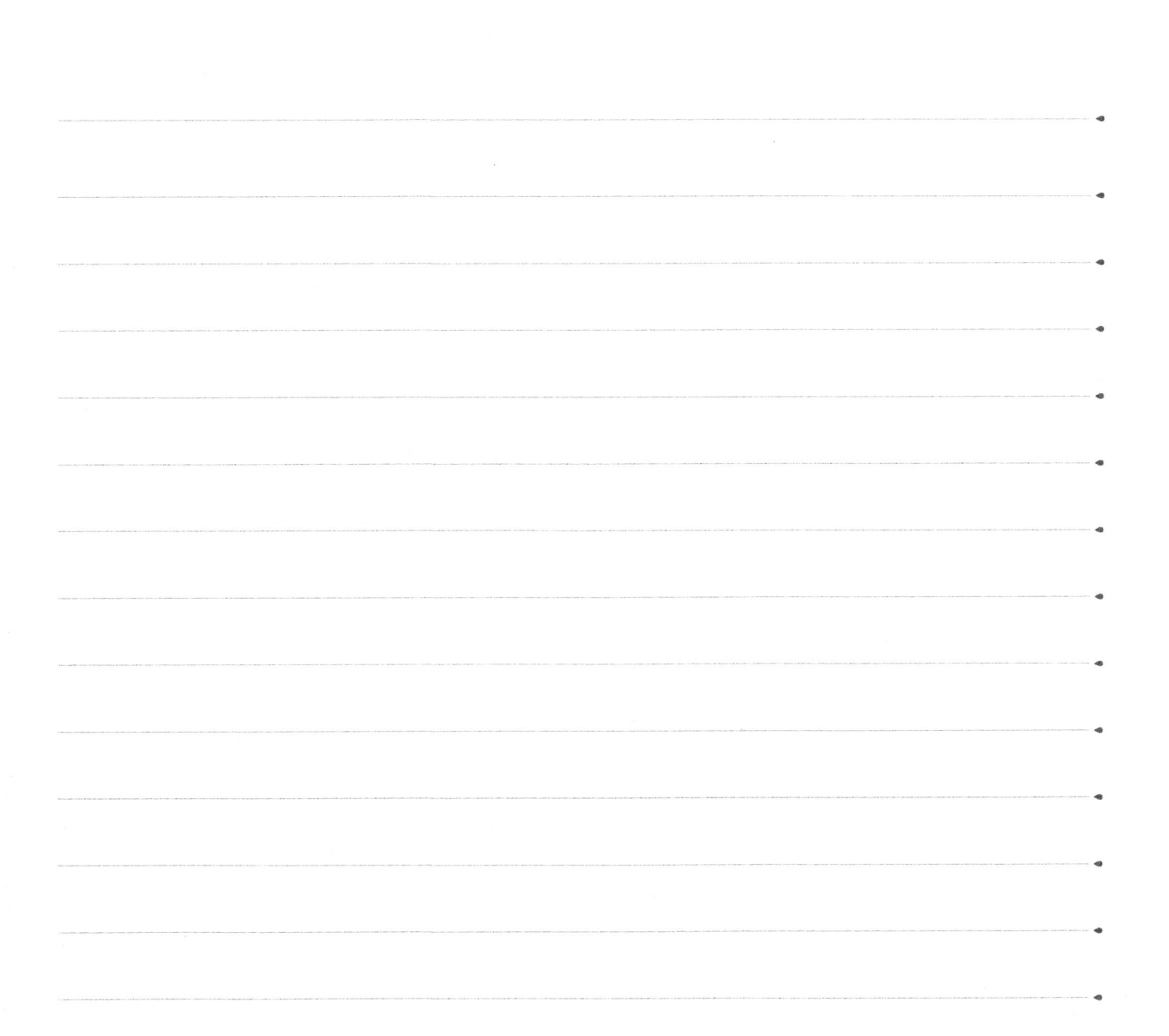

Beltane

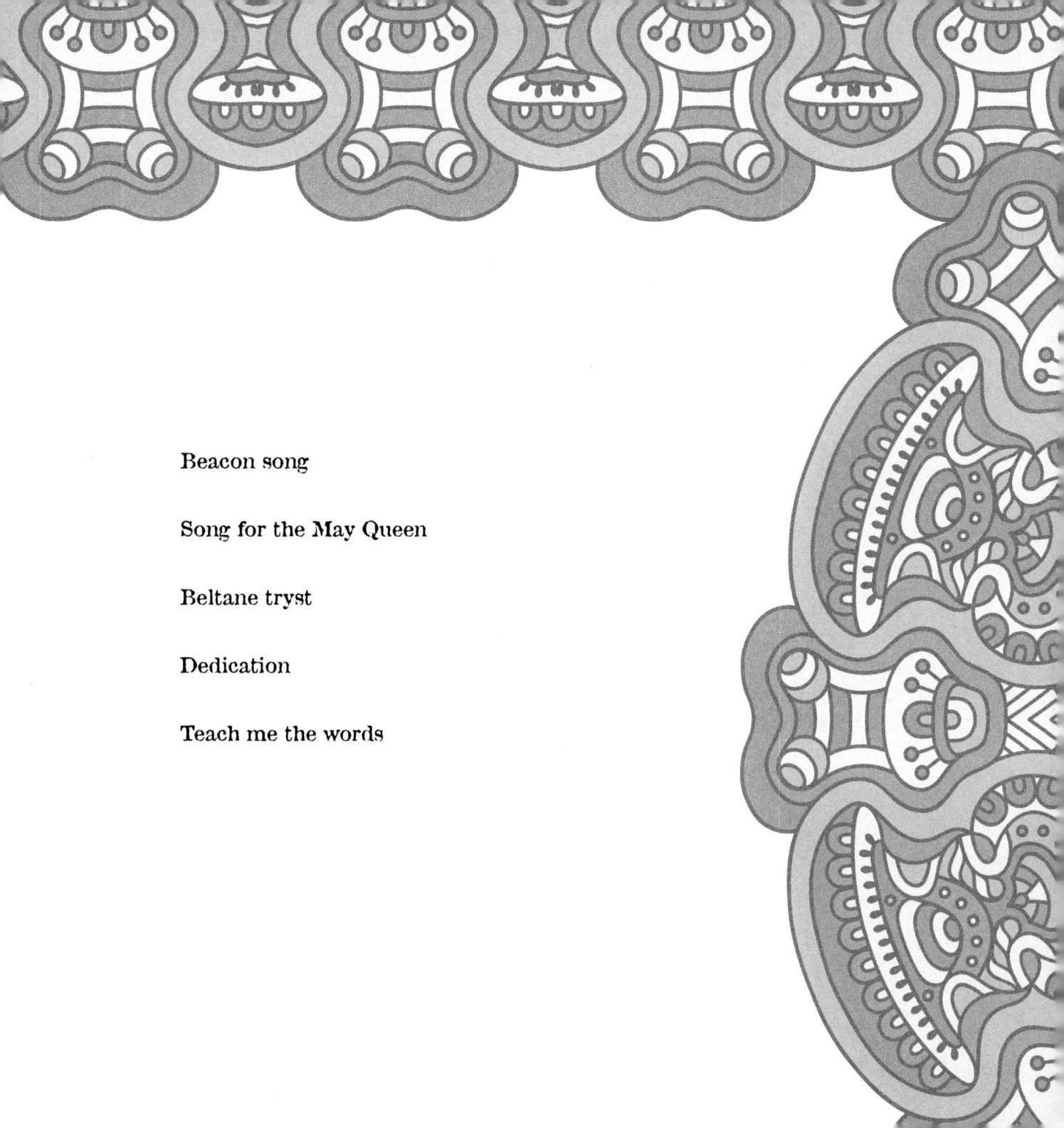

Beacon song

Song for the May Queen

Beltane tryst

Dedication

Teach me the words

Beacon song

Bright fire, bright fire, bright fire burn
Winter cold is fading
and summer will return

Bright fire, bright fire, bright fire dance
The nights are getting shorter;
we feel the year advance

Bright fire, bright fire, bright fire flare
Summer days are coming;
we sense it in the air

Bright fire, bright fire, bright fire spark
The sun's strength is returning
to banish the dark

Bright fire, bright fire, bright fire cleanse
We celebrate this season
with family and friends

Bright fire, bright fire, bright fire flame
We greet the coming summer
with music, song and games

Bright fire, bright fire, bright fire heal
Purify and strengthen
the people of the Wheel

Bright fire, bright fire, bright fire dance
The nights are getting shorter;
we feel the year advance

Bright fire, bright fire, bright fire burn
Winter cold is fading
and summer will return.

Song for the May Queen

*With a jangle of bells
and a stamping of feet,
with whistles and clapping
and a drum that we beat,
in fields and in forest
and in drab city street,
we welcome the Queen of the May*

We'll bathe in the dew
in the early dawn light,
then we'll crown her with roses,
pink, yellow and white.

We'll offer her nosegays
of blossom and bloom,
posies and pompoms,
lace, feather and plume.

We'll weave her a garland
set with jewels and treasure;
then, round with bright ribbons,
we'll dance for her pleasure.

*With a jangle of bells
and a stamping of feet,
with whistles and clapping
and a drum that we beat,
in fields and in forest
and in drab city street,
we welcome the Queen of the May.*

Beltane tryst

The forest is dark and the trees grow tall
but the grass between is sweet.
    I know that I'll find you waiting there
    when the Beltane fires are burning.

The forest is dark and the trees grow tall
and the peony blooms in the shade.
    Your horns are coarse and your breath is cool
    and the Beltane fires are burning.

The forest is dark and the trees grow tall;
mystery perfumes the air.
    All life holds its breath as I feel your touch
    when the Beltane fires are burning.

The forest is dark and the trees grow tall;
a sunbeam pierces the gloom.
    I lay you down and you gift me your love
    when the Beltane fires are burning.

The forest is dark and the trees grow tall;
the world is wild and new.
    We move as one in a frenzied dance
    while the Beltane fires are burning.

Dedication

I celebrate the source of light and life:
I honor the resplendent God
who showers his blessings on this world;
I honor the beneficent Goddess,
who blesses me with her abundance;
I recognize and honor the spirit within;
I honor the partnership of sun and earth
and the divine bond that unites us.

Teach me the words

The universe dances
her great choreography.
The universe sings as she spins.

Teach me the steps of the dance
Teach me the words of the song

I call upon the energizing sun,
whose constant heat and fire
quicken and inspire us to action
    Teach me the steps of the dance
    Teach me the words of the song

I call upon the cool and tender moon,
who bids the oceans follow her command
and draws our bodies to the tidal sway
    Teach me the steps of the dance
    Teach me the words of the song

I call upon the ever-watchful stars,
who write our fortunes in the night sky
and offer us hope beyond our little lives
    Teach me the steps of the dance
    Teach me the words of the song

I call upon the ever-changing rivers,
who carry the dross away
and show us the power of renewal
   Teach me the steps of the dance
   Teach me the words of the song

I call upon the green and fertile earth,
who nurtures all of us who dwell here
and nourishes us with her abundance
   Teach me the steps of the dance
   Teach me the words of the song

I call upon the patient, solid stones,
who have shared this stage through history
and will remain long after we are gone
   Teach me the steps of the dance
   Teach me the words of the song

The universe dances
her great choreography.
The universe sings as she spins.

Swing, spiral, whirl and waltz:
each of us plays our part.
Melody, harmony, counterpoint:
each of us has a voice.

The whole universe dances and sings.

My Beltane

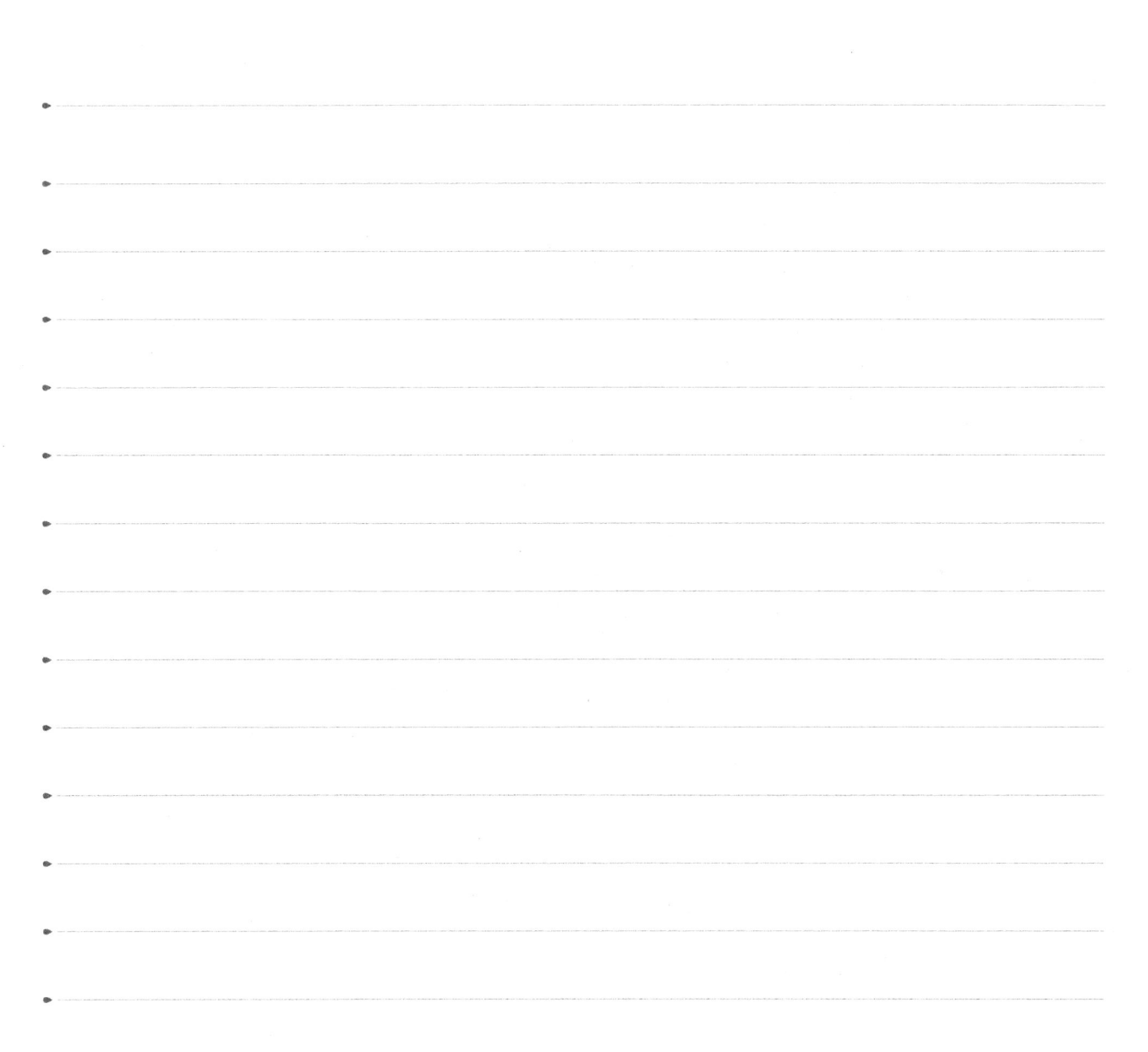

Litha

Song for the shortest night

Salutation

A witch's litany

A prayer to the ocean waves

A solstice request

Song for the shortest night

In the long days, we celebrate,
exulting in the healing warmth and light.
We find time to tread old paths
while sunflowers chaperone the idle hours.

In summer sun, the trees rejoice in green;
pansies, petunias and marigolds give voice
in vibrant color, shouting aloud
exuberant joy and candid pride in life.

In the brief hot nights, we dream
a tumble of magic and metamorphoses;
disjointed patchwork scenes collide
to show a myriad possibilities within our reach.

But shadows deepen in the long days:
we see our lives in stark relief.
Quick, now, before tomorrow brings the dark,
with racing hearts we revel in this moment.

Salutation

I lift my hands to the sky;
reaching towards the clouds,
I stretch my fingers wide.
My hands are small stars
anchored to the earth
by human limitations.

The sun's rays pierce
between my spread fingers
and my hands are clothed
in warmth and light.
Sunlight envelops
my whole being.

I stand on the earth
and stretch towards the sun.
And the sun reaches out
and sends his warmth and light
across the void of space
to embrace me here and now.

A witch's litany

No matter where I am,
I create my own footing.
I stand tall,
centered and grounded.

No matter the turmoil,
I create my own peace.
I am calm,
centered and grounded.

No matter the noise,
I create my own silence.
I am heard,
centered and grounded.

No matter the danger,
I create my own luck.
I am brave,
centered and grounded.

No matter the pain,
I create my own healing.
I am strong,
centered and grounded.

No matter what life brings,
I create my own existence.
I am powerful,
centered and grounded.

A prayer to the ocean waves

Come, soft tongues of the ocean,
as I bare my soul to you,
lick me clean of all my burdens.

Deafen me with your roar
and fill my ears with your salty voice,
for I am choked with the noise of the world.

Bathe my hands and arms
with your foamy tide
for I am weary from my labors.

Wash away the dust that has gathered
as I traveled the long path
that brings me to your sacred shore.

Play your drum on my chest
and cleanse my beaten heart
of the discord and hatred it has witnessed.

Kiss my eyes with your briny lips
that they may close themselves
to the chaos around me.

Knock and tumble me,
soft tongues of the ocean;
lick me clean of all my burdens
and give me rest.

A solstice request

The sun is high in the sky,
the days are long
and our world is warm
and welcoming.

We turn our faces up towards the light.
Yet we do not forget the other realms
and the mist that shimmers in the brief nights.

So if, by chance, wandering
among foxgloves and forget-me-nots,
we slip through the thin veil and intrude
into our neighbors' lands,
we ask that they take no offense,
but direct us to the road
that leads us home.

For the sun is high in the sky,
the days are long
and our world is warm
and welcoming.

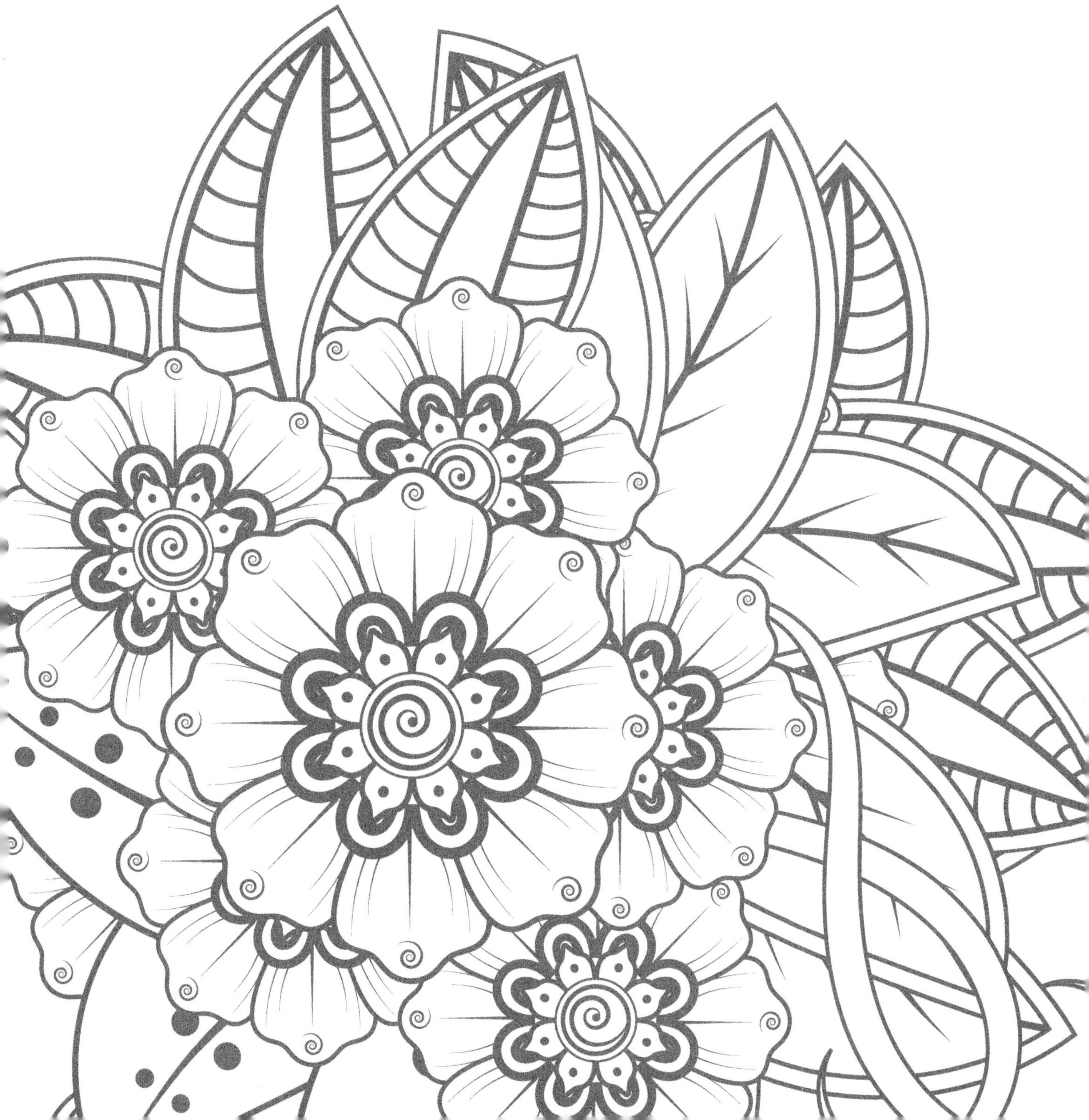

My Litha

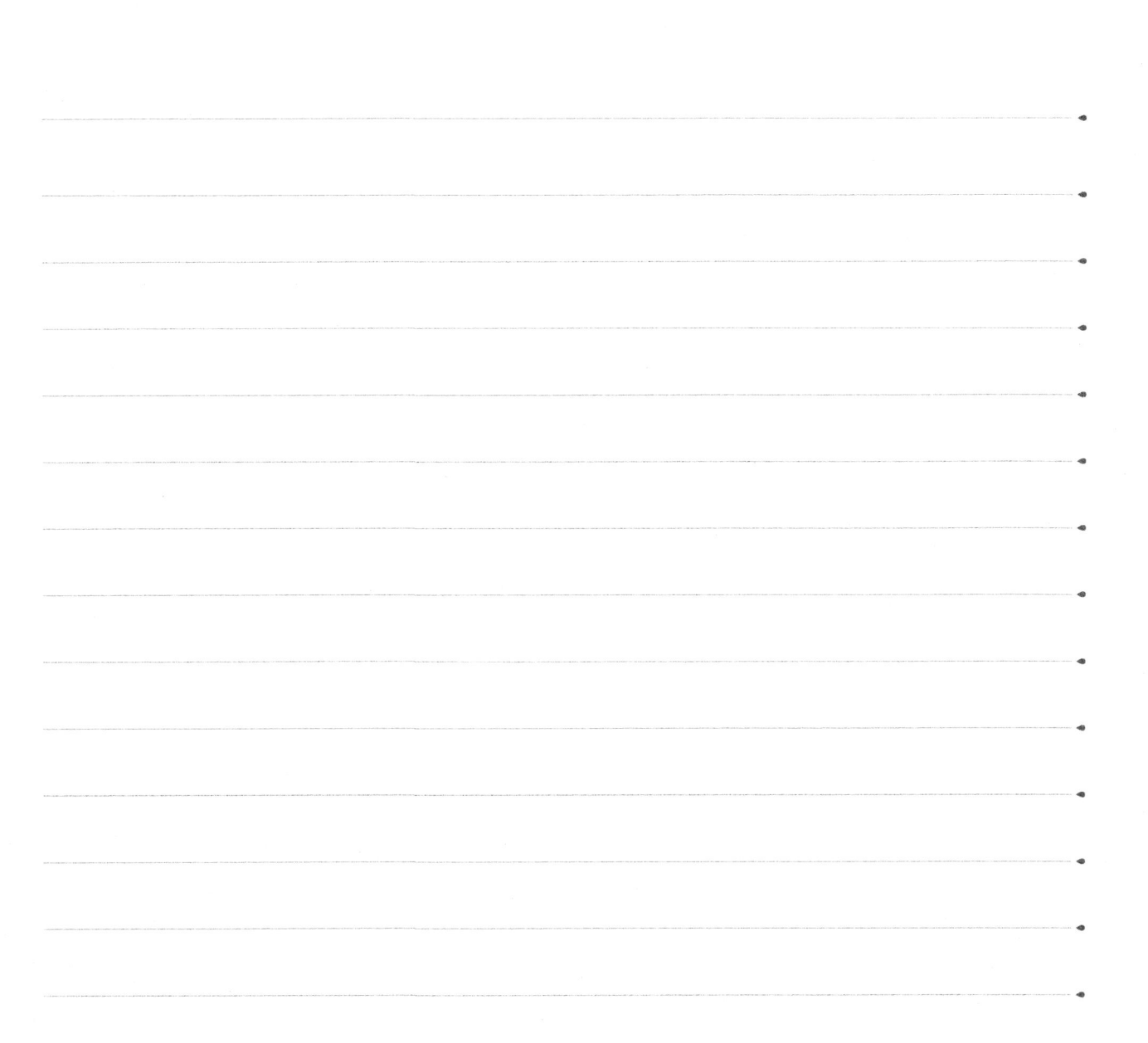

Lammas

My Lady's cloak

Stories

In honor of Lugh of the Long Hand

Kitchen witch

Trimming the dead wood

My Lady's cloak

Praise to the Goddess in her beauty

At dawn, my Lady's cloak is silver blue
edged with bright dew drops strung on spider silk.

My Lady's cloak at noon is golden bright;
like ripening wheat, the fabric flows and ripples through the fields.

My Lady's evening cloak is copper-red;
she spreads its folds and the whole world darkens like a bruise.

At night, my Lady wears a sable cloak
sequinned with stars and trimmed with quiet clouds.

Praise to the Goddess in her beauty

Stories

Buttercups punctuate
the scribbled tales
of meadow grasses

Slugs and snails drape
their chiffon yarns
across cool blue slate

Spiders scrawl
silken hieroglyphs
in dark angles

Dandelions interrupt
the clipped sentences
of well-kept corporation lawns

Let me listen and observe.
Then, let me tell my own story
with confidence and joy across the earth.

In honor of Lugh of the Long Hand

Lugh of the Long Hand,
skilled in many crafts,
sun-god and storm-god,
descendent of giants,
wielder of sling, sword and spear,
rider over land and sea,
Lugh of the Long Hand,
we honor you this Lammastide.

Lugh of the Long Hand,
skilled in many crafts,
who spared the life of Bres
to bring us the secrets
of farming the land –
when to plow, to sow, to reap,
Lugh of the Long Hand,
we honor you this Lammastide.

Lugh of the Long Hand,
skilled in many crafts,
we acknowledge your legacy
in modern agricultural machinery,
in the great combine harvesters
that reap and thresh, gather and winnow;
Lugh of the Long Hand,
we honor you this Lammastide.

Lugh of the Long Hand,
skilled in many crafts,
god of the cornfields,
we offer you fresh bread
and fruits from our gardens.
Lugh of the Long Hand,
skilled in many crafts,
we honor you this Lammastide.

Kitchen witch

I peel and slice, cut and grate,
chop and dice and trim;
I honor the long heritage of my ancestors.

    I step into my power.
    I am the artist creator, the potions master:
    I make brews, elixirs and philters,
       old favorites and new creations,
       justice and redress in every sip.

I grind and sift, crumble and blend,
pour and cream and fold;
I honor the tradition and legacy of generations.

    I step into my power.
    I live in abundance, I provide for all:
    I make hotpots, pies and cookies
       and share with family and neighbors,
       love and hope in every mouthful.

I peel and slice, cut and grate,
chop and dice and trim;
I grind and sift, crumble and blend,
pour and cream and fold.
I am the artist creator, the potions master;
I live in abundance, I provide for all.

Trimming the dead wood

I give thanks, this Lammastide, for the gifts of the earth;
I give thanks for the unending generosity of the planet.

I recognize that this is but a moment in the cycle:
there is work to be done if the harvest is to come again
and I acknowledge that I must play my part.
Now, at this moment of wealth and prosperity,
let me take time to look within:
    What fruit or gift will my life bring to the world?
    What must I do to fulfill my own potential?
    How can I grow and thrive and reach my full harvest?

As we mulch and feed the soil so the plants flourish,
let me seek out the right environment to encourage my growth.

As we cut away the dead wood to let in air and light to the heart of a tree,
let me cut away the unnecessary, the unhelpful, and the meaningless from my life.

As we prune unsound branches and remove diseased leaves,
let me give up unhealthy relationships that hold me back.

As we trim water shoots and suckers that divert a tree's energy,
let me give up old ideas and dreams that weaken my spirit.

As we thin disordered plants to restore their life and vigor,
let me cut away the distractions and bring focus to my life.

I give thanks, this Lammastide, for the gifts of the earth.
Let me cut away the dead wood from my own life
and work towards a better harvest for all.

My Lammas

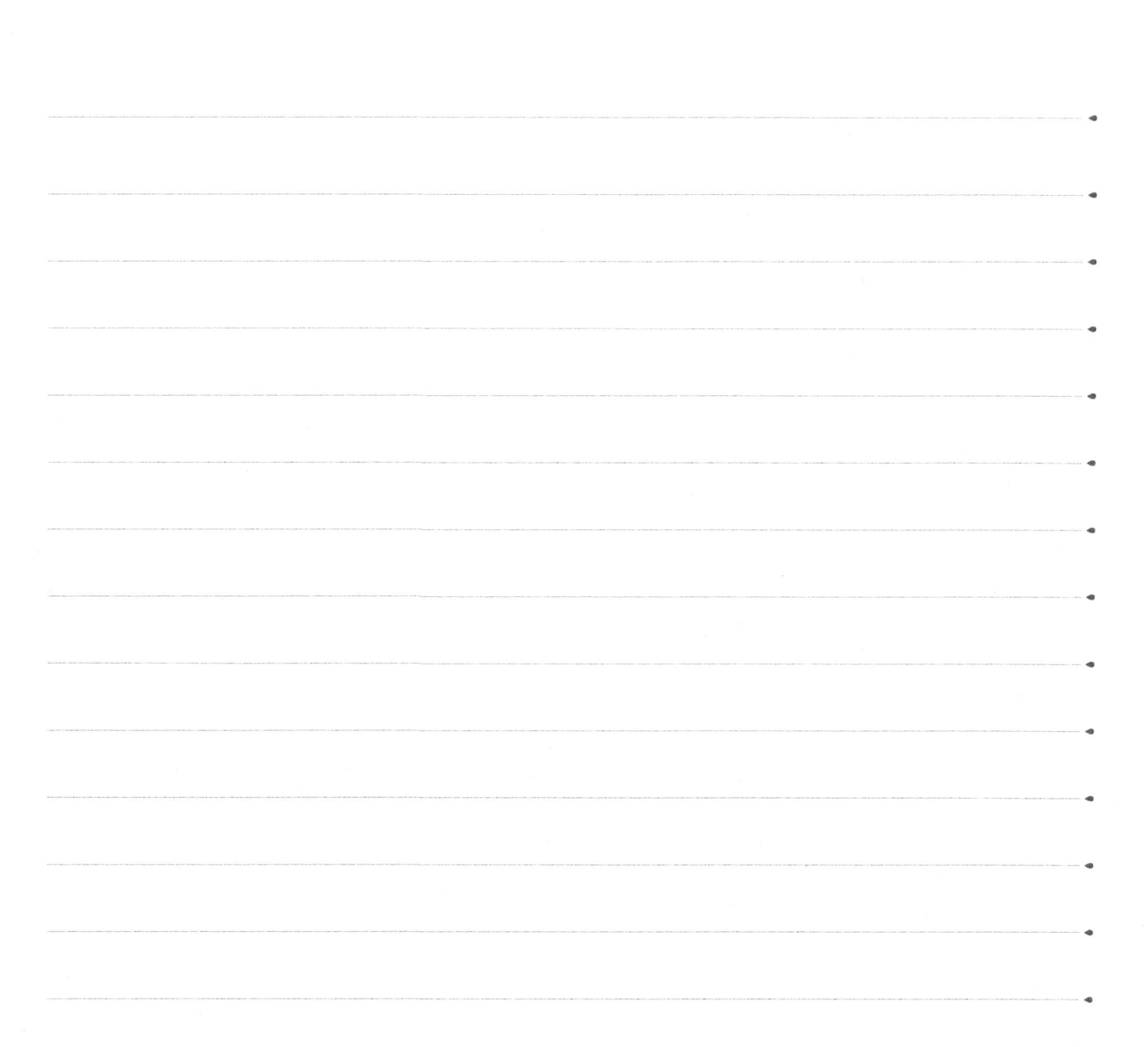

Mabon

As we approach the new school year

The world slips towards darkness

To Rosmerta the Most Providential

The fruit of wisdom

Harvest song for the Goddess

As we approach the new school year

The sun slips down towards fall and summer draws to a close.

We give thanks for the earth's abundance,
for gardens studded with bright autumn daisies,
for dull puddles that blaze with sudden sunlight,
and for trees turning to gold. Red, russet, purple,
berries and wild fruits twine through hedgerows;
we watch as those that dwell in the green
delight in their own harvest festival,
stocking their pantries against the coming cold.

Summer draws to a close and our thoughts turn to the new school year.

We give thanks for teachers and professors,
for school cooks and nurses, for janitors and admin staff;
for old friends reunited, and for new friends we haven't met yet.
We give thanks for new clothes and for hand-me-downs,
for new books and second-hand ones,
and for all the modern gadgetry that helps us learn.
We look ahead to winter, to gathering knowledge
and to learning; to sharing stories and secrets.

We will be curious, alert and questioning.
Later, we look forward to the harvest of the mind.

The world slips towards darkness

*Turning, the world slips down towards the dark;
summer nights shorten and the glad days grow dim.*

Looking back, we see the light recede.
The world decays, leaves fall and birdsong fades.
Ahead, the bleak grey winter beckons us.

The world slips towards darkness.

As the wheel turns and life slows,
let me look to the stable, centered core
and find comfort and strength within.

The world slips towards darkness.

Night follows day; the seasons come and go
in constant, certain sequence.
Our present seeps into the past.

*Turning, the world slips down towards the dark;
summer nights shorten and the glad days grow dim.*

To Rosmerta, the Most Providential

Generous Lady, Goddess Queen,
Great Provider, Bringer of Plenty,
we bless you and praise you;
we welcome your abundant gifts.

We thank you for your open-handedness,
for sharing with us unstintingly
from your limitless bounty.

Caring Lady, Goddess Queen,
within whose authority lie health and fertility,
we bless you and praise you;
we welcome your abundant gifts.

We thank you for our strength and energy,
for granting us physical and mental wellbeing
and for guiding those who care for us.

Prudent Lady, Goddess Queen,
Protector of Traders, Companion of Mercury,
we bless you and praise you;
we welcome your abundant gifts.

We thank you for sharing your wisdom
and for granting us acumen and competence
in our worldly schemes and business.

Lady Rosmerta, Goddess Queen,
generous, caring, prudent,
we bless you and praise you;
we welcome your abundant gifts.

The fruit of wisdom

In a field stood a tree
its branches heavy with apples;
then the harvesters came
and gathered the fruit

I hold an apple in my hand;
this apple is unique and so am I.
I ask the gods for understanding.

I hold an apple in my hand.
Its color – red, green, gold –
is made up of a myriad different shades;
tart or sweet, its flesh will nourish me.

But this apple was not made to feed me.
An apple is a tiny womb,
at its heart, a five-pointed star.
Each tight black seed
holds a promise of the future.

I hold an apple in my hand;
this apple is unique and so am I.
As the seed must go into the dark
to fulfill its destiny, so must the world.

I remember soft blossom
and the low hum of bees,
and I know that spring will come again.

I hold an apple in my hand
and ask the gods for patience.

In a field stood a tree
its branches heavy with apples;
then the harvesters came
and gathered the fruit.

Harvest song for the Goddess

You sit among us at the feast.
Your labor is done and it is time
to accept your due in quiet repose.

You hear the music,
but your feet are no longer nimble
and your voice is harsh and cracked.

But our songs and our dances
embody your memories
and we honor you.

The wheel turns
and the journey never ends.
May your wisdom guide us onward.

113

My Mabon

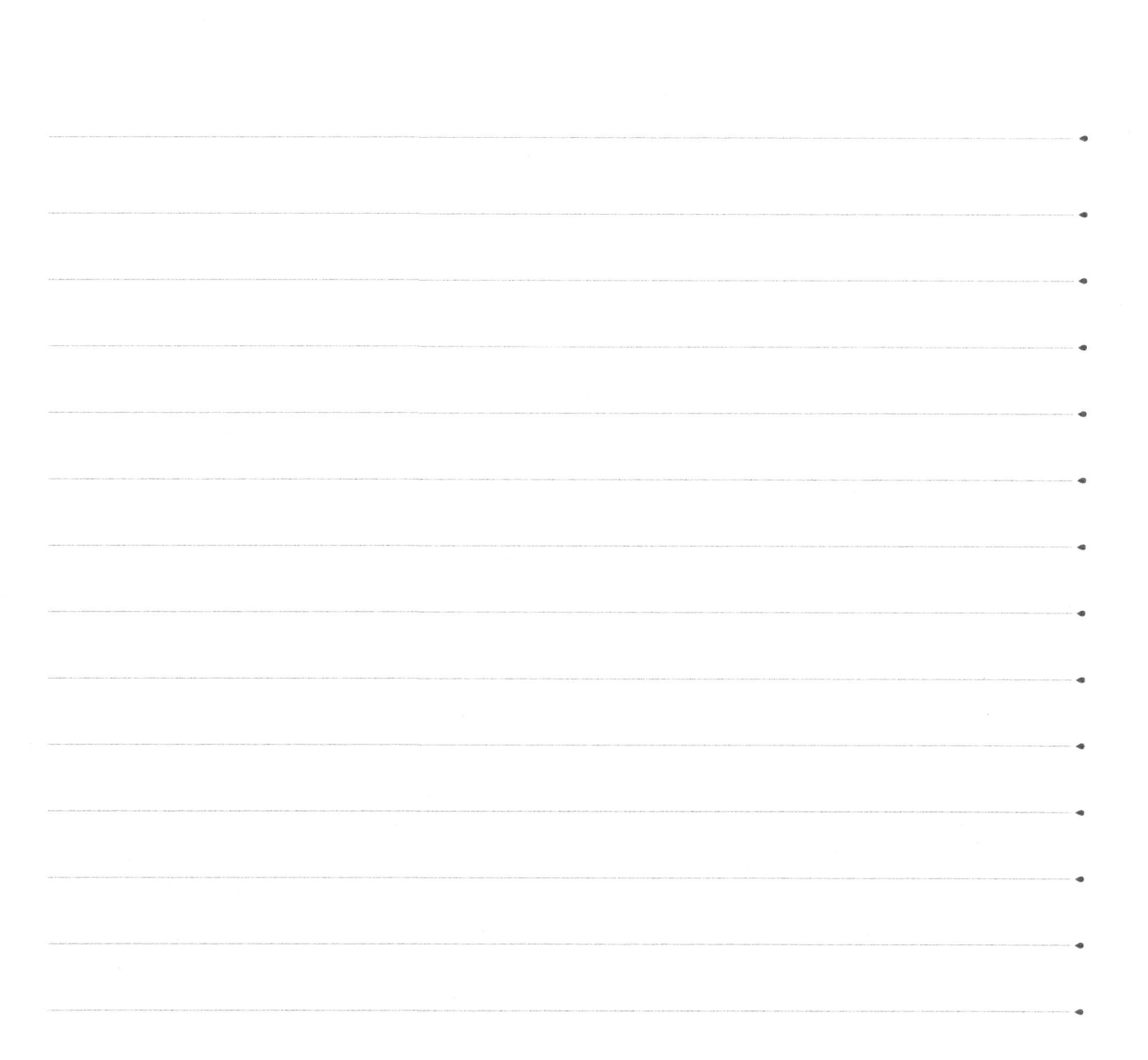

My Wheel of the Year

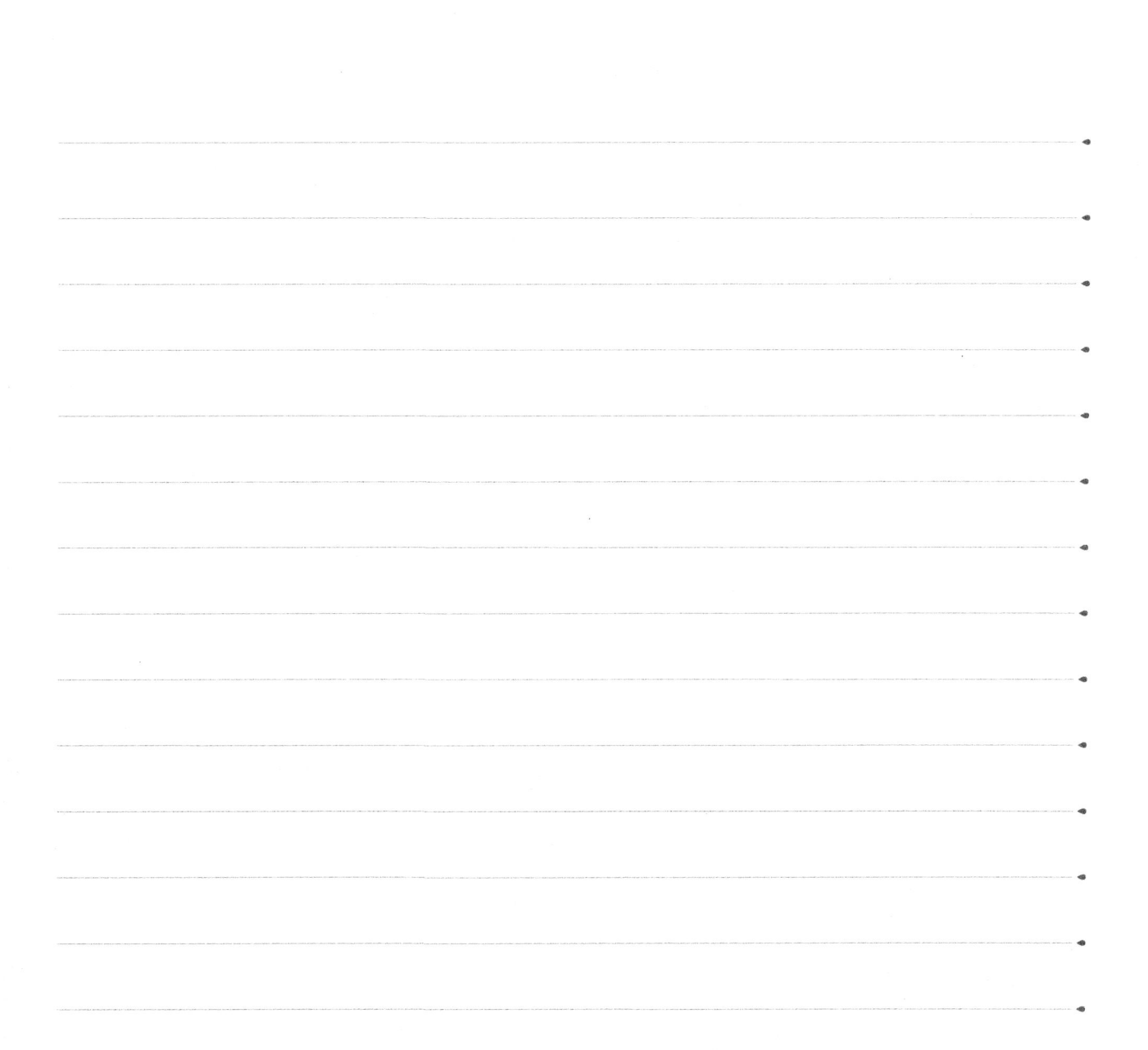

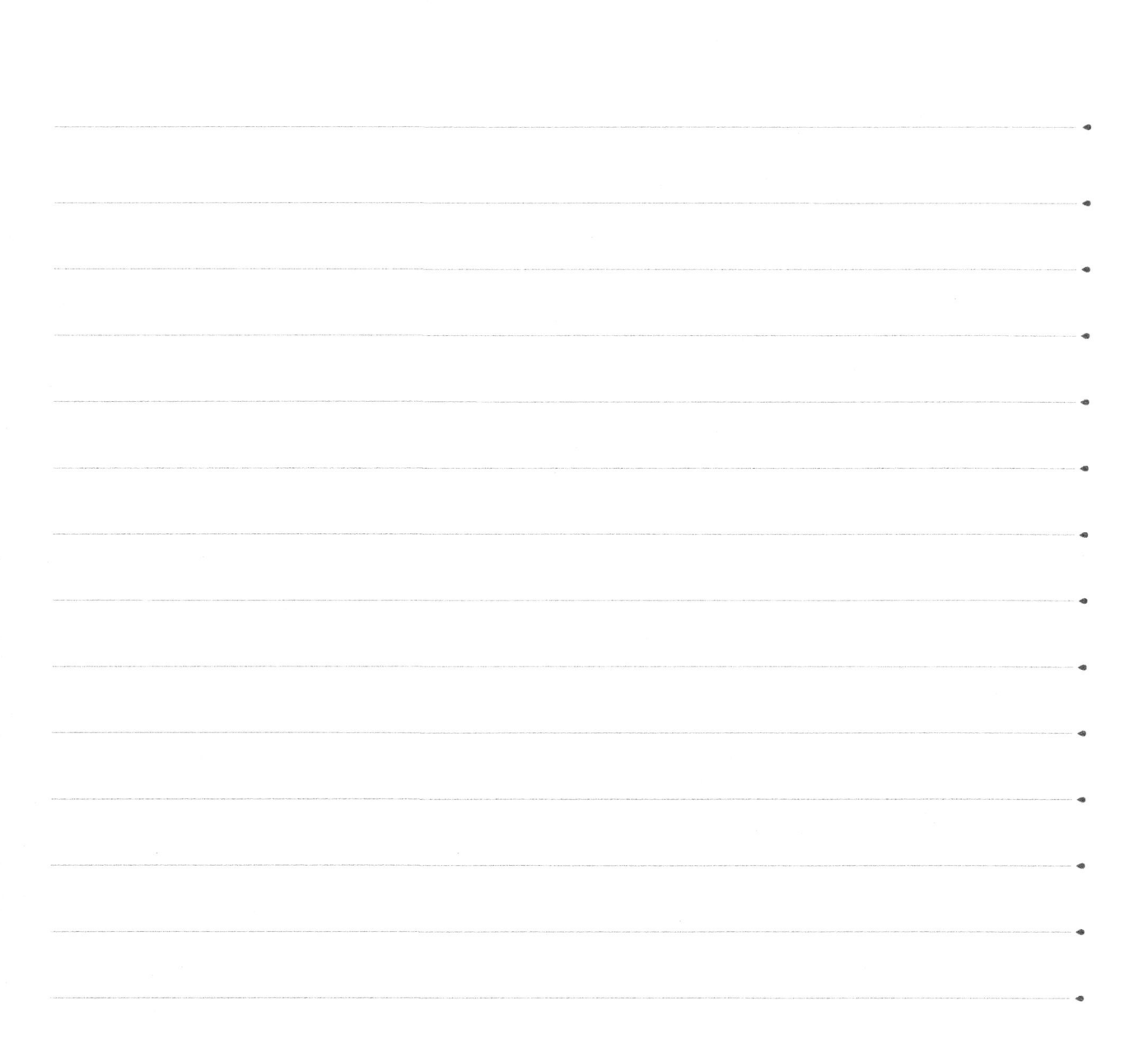

The authors

Lucía Moreno-Velo

Lucía is a Pantheist who believes Pagan theology can contribute to the conversation on justice and climate change. She lives with her wife and their two children in Madrid, Spain.

Gwyneth Box

Spiritually non-tribal, Gwyneth writes in many genres and is an award-winning poet. She leads workshops, mentors non-fiction writers and poets, and appears regularly at open mikes and on the radio.